MONSTER MUSIC FESTIVALS™

VANS WARPED TOUR

GREG ROBISON

rosen publishing's
rosen central®

New York

To Kelly Rae, my rock 'n' roll queen

Published in 2009 by The Rosen Publishing Group, Inc.
29 East 21st Street, New York, NY 10010

Copyright © 2009 by The Rosen Publishing Group, Inc.

First Edition

Library of Congress Cataloging-in-Publication Data

Robison, Greg.
Vans Warped Tour / Greg Robison.—1st ed.
    p. cm.—(Monster music festivals)
Includes bibliographical references (p. 46) and index.
ISBN-13: 978-1-4042-1754-6 (library binding)
ISBN-13: 978-1-4358-5119-1 (pbk)
ISBN-13: 978-1-4042-7864-6 (6 pack)
1. Vans Warped Tour—Juvenile literature. 2. Rock music festivals—Juvenile literature. I. Title.
ML36.V369 2009
781.66078'73—dc22

2007049640

Manufactured in Malaysia

On the cover: Foreground: Deryck Whibley of Sum 41 at the 2007 Vans Warped Tour in Kansas City, Kansas. Background, top row, left to right: Jorge Rodrigo Herrera of the Casualties at Uniondale, New York, 2006; "Fat Mike" Burkett of NOFX at Uniondale, 2006; the Aquabats at Fullerton, California, 2004; Maja Iversson of the Sounds at Uniondale, 2006. Background, left, top to bottom: Tim McIlrath of Rise Against at Uniondale, 2006; skateboarder in Orlando, Florida, 2003.

CONTENTS

INTRODUCTION

Mark Hoppus *(left)* of Blink-182 saw his band's popularity skyrocket after playing on the 1999 Vans Warped Tour. *(Above)* Crowd-surfers enjoy the Vans Warped Tour at the Shoreline Amphitheatre in Mountain View, California.

Take one hot summer day. Add approximately fourteen thousand screaming fans, one hundred bands on ten stages, and assorted pro skateboarders and BMX bikers. Throw in more than one hundred booths offering everything from food to "reverse daycare," where young moshers can check in their parents. Mix thoroughly. What's the result? The Vans Warped Tour!

The Warped Tour can best be described as a touring punk/new rock music and extreme sports festival. It's where musicians, athletes, and people of all different stripes come together to have a great time. The tour has introduced music fans to such artists as Blink-182, Eminem, No Doubt, Yellowcard, and Kid Rock. With more than fifty dates played annually across North America, chances are that a show will be coming to a place near you. You can catch performances by some of the hottest bands and extreme sports stars in the country. Also, you can find out who the "next big thing" will be on the Ernie Ball Stage, which features a national Battle of the Bands competition. Additionally, you don't want to miss the "Warped Are They Now?" exhibit—a traveling museum of past Warped Tour participants. As if that weren't enough, you can catch

the latest video games, download your favorite music from the Warped Music store, or create your own music and videos.

The Warped Tour celebrated its thirteenth year in 2007. It is the longest continuously running touring festival in the country, and it has repeatedly been voted the top summer festival by the readers of *Alternative Press*, a popular music magazine. Read on to find out what makes the Vans Warped Tour one of the most anticipated shows of the summer.

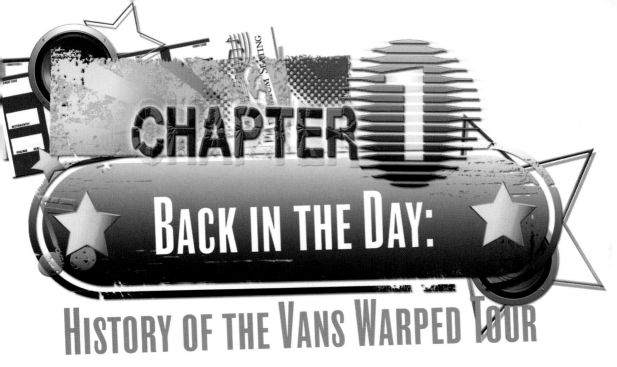

CHAPTER 1

BACK IN THE DAY:

HISTORY OF THE VANS WARPED TOUR

I f you have the opportunity to meet Kevin Lyman, founder of the Vans Warped Tour, chances are that you will be reminded of the Energizer Bunny. Like the famous drumming rabbit, Lyman just keeps going and going.

Meet Kevin Lyman

Kevin Lyman is best known as the creator and producer of the wildly successful Vans Warped Tour. However, he is also involved in additional business ventures. His company, 4Fini, Inc., has created other successful tours, including the Watcha Tour, Down From the Mountain Tour, Sprite Tour, and the Great High Mountain Tour. Lyman recently launched the Taste of Chaos Tour, featuring some of the biggest names on the hardcore/screamo scene. 4Fini also consults for corporations,

The main man. Kevin Lyman, founder of the Vans Warped Tour, oversees all aspects of the tour, making sure things are running smoothly.

helping them to maintain "street credibility" so that their products are noticed and purchased by young consumers.

If that weren't enough, Lyman is also part owner of SideOneDummy Records, an independent record label known for its impressive and diverse artist roster. Still, Lyman somehow finds the time to teach music business classes at a community college in California.

Lyman began his career in the music industry by booking bands for his college and working as a road crew member for such up-and-coming bands as the Untouchables, the Bangles, and Bad Religion. After college, Lyman began working with the independent concert promoter Goldenvoice. There, he served as production manager for punk rock and metal greats, including the Germs, Metallica,

Anthrax, and Jane's Addiction. With all of that experience to back him up, Lyman decided to form his own production company, Kevin Lyman Production Services. No stranger to hard work, he put on an unbelievable 318 shows in one year. As Lyman quips in *Warped Book: Tales of Freedom and Psychotic Ambition*, "I was working so much, it was keeping me out of trouble . . . I had to be the guy up in the morning buying the catering for the next day's show, getting things started at nine or ten in the morning, and working until two AM. I stayed grounded by living out in Claremont. Everyone told me that I couldn't make it in the business unless I moved to Hollywood, but it kept me straight."

This turned out to be an excellent choice, as bigger and better things were just around the corner for Lyman.

Bands, Boards, and Bikes: Bringing It All Together

Lyman conceived of the Warped Tour in 1994, along with attorney David Codikow and music agents Rick Roskin and Daryl Eaton. Lyman was familiar with both the extreme sports world and the music world, having worked on skateboard expos such as the Vision Skate Escape and Holiday Havoc. He also had a hand in the very first Lollapalooza tour in 1991, working in production, security, and as a stage manager. Lyman calls his involvement with the 1992 Lollapalooza tour the greatest experience of his life. It gave him the opportunity to

Working with great bands like the Red Hot Chili Peppers on the Lollapalooza tour *(above)* gave Kevin Lyman the experience he needed to start the Vans Warped Tour.

work with the hottest musical artists in the world, and it also taught him the importance of keeping an eye out for emerging artists and extreme sports athletes.

The Warped Tour idea first came to Lyman while he was helping to organize Board Aid, a music festival sponsored by *Transworld Magazine*. *Transworld*'s specialty is covering extreme sports such as skateboarding, surfing, and BMX riding. Board

Aid brought together bands, boarders, and fans from all over the country to spread social awareness and support charitable organizations. Top artists including the Offspring, the Specials, and Wyclef Jean participated in these events. Board Aid inspired Lyman to take that festival formula on the road in the form of the Warped Tour.

In 1995, the first official Warped Tour hit the road, with eighteen bands, assorted skaters, and Lyman. The idea was to entertain the fans and give them the opportunity to interact with the bands and athletes. That first Warped Tour played in twenty-five cities and was anything but easy. In fact, the tour actually lost money. However, in spite of all the challenges, both Lyman and the concert promoters saw great potential, as more and more kids were showing up for the shows each day.

In an interview published on the Music Edge, a Web site run by the National Association of Music Merchants, Lyman remembers, "We definitely pulled it together in 1995, which was great, but we barely made it that first year. People saw the hard work that we put into it, however, and how committed we were." All of that hard work was about to pay off in a big way.

A Better Name

Originally, Lyman wanted to call his new tour The Bomb. However, the morning that the tour was to be announced,

Vans sneakers are a favorite among extreme sports athletes and musicians—and their fans, as well.

the Oklahoma City bombing tragedy occurred. Lyman decided it would be best to change the name. So, at the last minute, he called the folks at *Warped Magazine* and received permission to use the name "Warped Tour."

Vans Signs On

Since 1966, when Paul Van Doren founded the Van Doren Rubber Co., Vans has succeeded in introducing the "California style" to the rest of the world. Vans shoes, apparel, and accessories are specifically designed for fans of today's extreme sports culture, which includes skateboarding, BMX bikes, and snowboarding. The company's unflagging commitment to tracking the latest trends has made its brand the one of choice for young and active consumers all around the world.

In 1996, Vans president and CEO Gary Schoenfeld wanted to launch an amateur skate contest to find the best skateboarders in the world. He contacted Lyman for help with this event. For Lyman, the meeting could not have come at a better time. "I was desperate for money to keep the tour going," he recalls. "At this point, I was literally taking money out of the coin jar to pay my bills." When they met, Lyman persuaded Schoenfeld that adding music would bring the people to the contest, and he suggested that they put the amateur contest on the Warped Tour. The CEO loved the idea, and by the next day, Vans signed on as the title sponsor of the tour. Since then, it has been known as the Vans Warped Tour.

Something for Everyone

Being the longest-running touring festival in North America is no small accomplishment. What is it that separates the Vans Warped Tour from other shows? In the Music Edge interview, Lyman gives his perspective. "We try and keep things fresh," he explains. "We try and find what's most popular with the kids at the time. For example, when I first saw freestyle motocross, I went out and built some ramps, and before the public even knew who they were, I brought out Brian Deegan, Carey Hart, and Ronnie Faisst. They came out and jumped freestyle at Warped way before most or any of the kids had seen it at X Games. We just try to stay a little bit ahead of the curve,

The Vans Warped Tour gives you a chance to check out some of the biggest names in extreme sports, such as freestyle motocross rider Carey Hart.

but not mess around with it too much."

Having a corporate sponsor like Vans doesn't hurt either. A corporate sponsor is a company that agrees to provide money or its product to an organization in order to help pay the costs of an event. In return, the sponsor gets to display its name everywhere at the event, including on posters, T-shirts, and stages. Corporate sponsorship helps keep the ticket and merchandising prices low, thus allowing more kids the chance to experience the Vans Warped Tour.

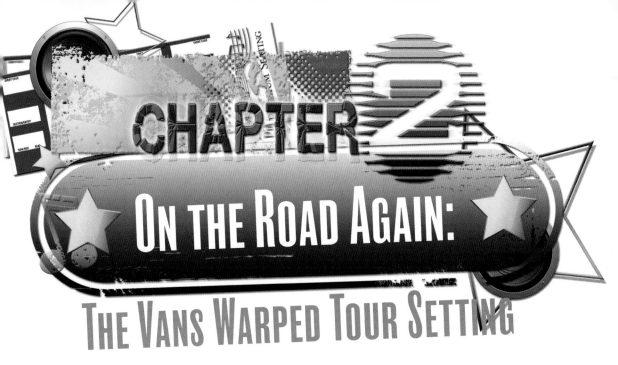

CHAPTER 2

ON THE ROAD AGAIN:

THE VANS WARPED TOUR SETTING

Why is the Vans Warped Tour so great? The reasons are almost too many to list. But for starters, you get to see almost one hundred bands for less than thirty dollars. That's a lot of music for just a little money!

Where the Vans Warped Tour Takes Place

The Vans Warped Tour is an all-inclusive show, or a "tour in a box." The sound system, lights, musical equipment, stages, skate and bike ramps, merchandise, vendor and concession booths, and, of course, the bands and extreme sports athletes all travel with the tour. This makes it much easier to set up virtually anywhere—at music halls, coliseums and athletic stadiums, large outdoor parking lots, and even in pastures and fields. On the 2007 tour, you could have checked out the

Howard Jones, lead vocalist of heavy metal band Killswitch Engage, rocks the crowd in Pomona, California, the first stop of the Vans Warped Tour 2007.

Pomona, California, show at the Pomona Fairplex, or at the Race City Speedway in Alberta, Canada. If you were in Denver, Colorado, Invesco Field at Mile High Stadium was where you were rocking.

The Vans Warped Tour brings new meaning to the phrase "road trip." It generally begins in the middle of June and runs through the middle of August, winding its way through the

United States and much of Canada. In 2006, an incredible fifty shows were played in fifty-nine days to more than 750,000 fans across North America. The tour has also traveled abroad, playing dates in Europe, Japan, Australia, and New Zealand.

Punk Rock Traveling Circus: What to See and Do

If you are going to attend the Vans Warped Tour, plan on coming early and staying late. Below are a few tips and reminders that will help make your tour experience even more fun:

- Make sure you have enough money for food, drinks, and a souvenir or two.
- If you don't want to bring a lot of cash, most of the tour vendors accept major credit cards, and they usually have an ATM machine on site as well.
- Don't forget your cell phone, or change for a pay phone, in case you need to call someone, or they need to call you.
- Check the weather before you leave your house. If it's going to be hot, don't forget the sunscreen and a hat. If it looks like rain, you might want to stash an extra T-shirt and shorts in your backpack. Wear comfortable shoes because you will be doing a lot of walking around.

The Vans Warped Tour takes place during the summer, so things can really heat up. Here, parched fans get relief from a makeshift water fountain at the 2004 tour stop in Montana.

- If you don't drive, make sure your ride knows when and where to pick you up after the show.

From the moment you walk in the gate, you'll notice that there's something for everyone to enjoy. First things first: If you come with your folks, you can check them in at the Reverse Daycare tent. This is a comfortable waiting area where parents and guardians can hang out while you check out the tour's attractions. Watch the pro/am skateboard exhibition on the half-pipe, along with some incredible BMX stunt riders. Play the latest video games. Shop at the vendor booths. Learn about different organizations and charitable foundations. Take a break from the mosh pit and cool off in one of the misting tents. Grab a snack from one of the various food vendors. You can even meet your favorite band or extreme athlete. Many vendors, record labels, and tour sponsors host "meet and greets," where bands come to their booths to sign autographs and greet their fans. And let's not forget the live music. Everywhere you look, there is a band playing at the Warped Tour.

The Sounds of the Vans Warped Tour

One reason the Vans Warped Tour is so popular is that it appeals to such a diverse audience. If you're a fan of punk, alternative, rap, ska, or reggae music, chances are good that your favorite band has played on the tour.

Tour founder Kevin Lyman has the final say regarding all bands on the tour. He has his own preferences, but he also pays close attention to what the fans have to say. "I get on the Internet and MySpace now as well," he says, "and see what bands the kids are talking about. I'll track down bands that I get turned on to, and have them send me their music." Regular fans can also give their input by going to the Warped Tour's Internet voting

Here are guitarist Josh Farro and singer Hayley Williams of Paramore. The alternative rockers were fan favorites during the Vans Warped Tour 2007.

system to select the bands that they would like to see play an additional ten minutes at each show.

In addition to punk and alternative bands, the tour has featured hundreds of other bands from different musical genres, including metal, emo, goth, rockabilly, and even country.

With more than one hundred bands performing each day, it takes a huge amount of planning and hard work to get the Warped Tour up and running. Setup generally begins around six AM, a time of day when some bands are just getting to bed! Tour personnel quickly assemble stages, sound systems, and lights, while organizers get together to arrange the daily performance schedule. Most bands perform for thirty minutes, with set times rotating on a daily basis. Performance times are from 11:00 AM to 9:00 PM each day.

In order for one hundred bands to play each day, there are stages everywhere on the Vans Warped Tour. The two main stages are set up side by side. So, while one band is playing on one stage, another band is setting up on the other stage. And when one band is finished playing, the next band on the other stage is ready to go immediately. The arrangement lets bands play on the main stages around the clock.

Beyond the main stages, there are more than a dozen smaller stages, located throughout the tour grounds. Some

Vans Warped Tour Bands

Some of the biggest bands in the world have taken a turn on the Warped Tour music stages. Do you see any of your favorites on this list?

311	My Chemical Romance
AFI	Simple Plan
Black Eyed Peas	Social Distortion
Blink-182	Story of the Year
Dropkick Murphys	Sublime
Eminem	Taking Back Sunday
Good Charlotte	Underoath
Joan Jett and the Blackhearts	Weezer
Limp Bizkit	Hank Williams III

bands will even set up in the parking lot or near a vendor booth and crank it up! There is no shortage of great music on the Vans Warped Tour.

Impact on the Environment

Clearly, the organizers of the Vans Warped Tour are focused on exposing people to great music. But they are also into raising awareness of environmental issues. In fact, with its Warped Eco-Initiative, the Vans Warped Tour is one of the most environmentally friendly shows out there.

In 2006, the tour made the smart decision to convert all of its vehicles to run on biodiesel fuel. With seventeen tour buses and nineteen production trucks on the road for two months, the tour consumes a lot of fuel. By switching to biodiesel fuel, the tour utilizes renewable natural resources and produces a lot less pollution than it would using regular fuels.

Everyone involved with the tour is encouraged to reduce, reuse, and recycle. In select cities, volunteers who help in this effort can gain free access to the show, a T-shirt, and other Vans Warped Tour items.

Giving Back

Check out any stop on the Vans Warped Tour, and you will see numerous vendors set up in booths, creating an open-air market

The main stage on the Vans Warped Tour always attracts huge crowds. These fans are enjoying one of the many bands performing on the main stage in Pompano Beach, Florida.

atmosphere. Among these vendors you might find civil rights and environmental groups, as well as anti-racism organizations.

In addition, numerous charities benefit from the tour each year. These include the National Hopeline Network, 1-800-SUICIDE, and other teen suicide hotlines. A tent called Girlz Garage devised a unique way to support suicide hotlines. Fans who visit the tent design their own T-shirts and bid on Vans

shoes designed by bands on the tour. The proceeds from both the T-shirts and the shoes go directly to the suicide hotlines.

The tour also benefits the American Red Cross, as well as leukemia, cancer, and AIDS research centers. For every four tickets sold, the Warped Tour donates a dollar to Camp Hollywood Heart, a camp for kids and families affected by HIV/AIDS.

In 2005, the Vans Warped Tour donated $300,000 to Habitat for Humanity, a contribution that paid directly for the construction of five new houses for victims of Hurricane Katrina. Not content just to donate money, various performers from the tour came together to build a prefabricated home, which was then shipped to Louisiana and given to a family in need.

The Vans Warped Tour offers you affordable tickets, almost one hundred bands, amazing skaters and BMX riders, something for everyone to see and do, and the chance to give back. When it comes to having fun and getting involved, you would be hard-pressed to improve on the Vans Warped Tour formula.

CHAPTER 3

MAKING IT HAPPEN:

THE PEOPLE OF THE VANS WARPED TOUR

One thing's for certain—there's no shortage of people involved with the Vans Warped Tour. More than 750,000 North American fans attended the tour in 2006, and that figure doesn't even include the bands, extreme sports athletes, and tour personnel that travel with the tour, or the folks who work at the local venues.

Making It Happen:
The People and Jobs on the Vans Warped Tour

We all know about the jobs of the musicians and athletes on the Vans Warped Tour. However, there are many other important folks on the tour as well, people who toil every day to make it happen. In fact, a total of nearly four hundred people travel with the tour. Who are these people? And what do they do?

Tour Bus/Semi Driver

There are at least seventeen band buses on the tour, twelve production buses, and ten eighteen-wheeler semitrucks, not to mention additional tour vehicles. It takes great drivers to get the tour from one place to another. Tour drivers log anywhere from 200 to 500 miles (322 to 805 kilometers) per night. They often sleep during the day and drive all night because the tour usually begins setting up at 6:00 AM each day.

Tour Nurse Practitioner

Do you think your school nurse is busy? Imagine being responsible for all of the bands, crews, and athletes on the Vans Warped Tour. The tour nurse practitioner typically passes out more than one thousand packages of Band-Aids and empties more than five giant bottles of aspirin each tour. Additionally, the nurse practitioners treat more serious injuries, like one suffered by a tour motocross rider who missed the ramp and caught the gearshift in his neck. Ouch!

Tour Caterer

Can you imagine having to cook for more than four hundred people several times a day? The caterer's mobile kitchen travels in its own eighteen-wheeler, which houses eight ovens, three grills, an eight-burner stove, four sinks, and a huge walk-in freezer. So, the tour caterer is prepared for almost anything.

The caterer serves up to 150 pounds (68 kilograms) of meat per day!

Production Engineer

When you have nearly one hundred bands from different genres performing on more than ten stages, it's a real challenge getting them all to sound their best. Production engineers are usually located behind the giant soundboards in front of the stage. They are responsible for mixing the bands' music, checking the volume levels of all the instruments and microphones, and making sure the bands sound great for their fans.

Extreme athletes go all out on the Vans Warped Tour. The tour nurse practitioner and the first-aid team are close by in case the athletes get banged up.

Tour Security

It's important that both the bands onstage and the fans in the mosh pit are safe at all times. The Vans Warped Tour employs

You can expect big crowds—along with giant mosh pits—on the Vans Warped Tour. Alert tour security personnel (yellow shirts, above) make sure that the fun doesn't get out of hand.

more than seventy security guards a day to ensure that everyone has an experience that's both fun and safe.

Merchandise Vendor

Most people who come to the Vans Warped Tour want to purchase a souvenir to remember the awesome time they had. It may be a T-shirt or a CD from their favorite band, a cool skateboard deck, or one of the other unique items available at the vendor booths. Merchandise vendors are responsible for setting up and taking down their booths each day.

Road Crew Member

Road crew members, or "roadies," wear a lot of different hats. Their job duties include loading musical equipment on and off stage, tuning instruments, and setting up and breaking down lighting rigs. In addition, they are usually on hand

Keeping musical instruments in good shape is just one of the many duties that road crew members perform each day.

during the band's show in case someone breaks a guitar string or drumstick, or needs a towel or bottled water.

First-Aid Tent Personnel

If you are dehydrated from overdoing it in the mosh pit, or if you have a minor scrape or cut that needs attention, the good

folks at the first-aid tent are there to help you out. Always open during the show, they can treat minor injuries or just offer fans a place to lie down and cool off until they are ready to rock again.

Tour Clean-Up Personnel

The time is 9:00 PM, and you are headed for the exits after a long, fun-filled day. This is when the clean-up crew is getting ready to go to work. Each festival produces more than 4 tons (4,000 kilograms) of trash. Do these folks a favor and dispose of your trash properly as you leave.

After a Vans Warped Tour show in Massachusetts, these volunteers collected fifteen giant bags of recyclable plastic bottles. They earned free Warped Tour passes for their hard work.

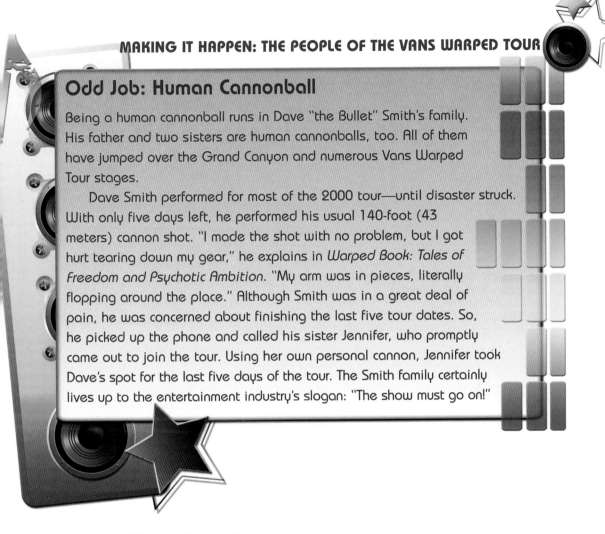

Odd Job: Human Cannonball

Being a human cannonball runs in Dave "the Bullet" Smith's family. His father and two sisters are human cannonballs, too. All of them have jumped over the Grand Canyon and numerous Vans Warped Tour stages.

Dave Smith performed for most of the 2000 tour—until disaster struck. With only five days left, he performed his usual 140-foot (43 meters) cannon shot. "I made the shot with no problem, but I got hurt tearing down my gear," he explains in *Warped Book: Tales of Freedom and Psychotic Ambition*. "My arm was in pieces, literally flopping around the place." Although Smith was in a great deal of pain, he was concerned about finishing the last five tour dates. So, he picked up the phone and called his sister Jennifer, who promptly came out to join the tour. Using her own personal cannon, Jennifer took Dave's spot for the last five days of the tour. The Smith family certainly lives up to the entertainment industry's slogan: "The show must go on!"

Over Half a Million Strong: Who Attends the Vans Warped Tour

In their song "The Rock Show," Blink-182 proclaims, "We couldn't wait for the summer and the Warped Tour!" A lot of other people from across the country feel the same way. Since 2004, the tour has entertained an average of more than 700,000

fans per tour throughout North America. Generally, the tour attracts about 14,500 attendees per date, with approximately forty-five to forty-nine dates per tour.

Who makes up all of these people who come out to the show? People ages fifteen to twenty-one make up 80 percent of the audience. Further breakdown shows that males and females show up in just about equal numbers. Whether you are a student in middle school, high school, or college, or you are an adult who likes to rock, you're welcome on the tour. The Vans Warped Tour is an all-ages event. Tour attendees are generally media-savvy, tech-loving music fans who are looking for the latest and greatest sounds, trends, and products.

Many fans of the Warped Tour may not be able to make it out to one of the live tour dates. However, they can still follow the tour, as it always receives a tremendous amount of media coverage. On television, tune in to Fuse, MTV, CNN, Musique Plus, Much Music (Canada's Music Channel), ESPN X, 2-Day, and Fox Sports Net for updates and coverage. Also, network news stations regularly run features about the tour. Read about your favorite Warped Tour band in *Rolling Stone*, *Alternative Press*, *Spin*, *Billboard*, *Time*, *Teen People*, *Newsweek*, and *GQ* magazines, or check out newspapers like *USA Today* and the *New York Times*. Or, you can surf the Internet to stay up to date. Check out the Web sites for Allstar, MySpace, Fanscape, Billboard Online, MTV Online, Spin, Pollstar, and, of course, the Warped Tour.

CHAPTER 4

A Day in the Life:

Experiencing the Vans Warped Tour

The Vans Warped Tour is not just a show. For many people, it has become an annual tradition. Among musicians, it's fondly known as "Punk Rock Summer Camp," and many bands cite Warped Tour as their favorite tour experience of all time. Fans plan summer vacations around the tour dates that they want to attend, and some even follow the tour from city to city. Folks employed by the tour work very hard, but they find time to have a lot of fun as well. Read on to see what kind of experiences these people have had.

The Fan's Experience

Jeff Maguire is a skater and an old-school punk rock fan. Growing up in California and Texas, he skated to the sounds of Social Distortion, Hüsker Du, X, Rancid, and Sublime. He

remembers his very first Warped Tour. "It was the first tour that went out in 1996," he recalls. "I was at the Houston, Texas, date at the Astrohall arena. It was indoors, and there were probably about 2,000 kids there. Sublime, No Use for a Name, Sick of It All, and Guttermouth completely ripped it up! Steve Alba, Mike Frazier, and a bunch of other pro skaters tore up the half-pipe." Since then, Maguire hasn't missed many Texas dates. What's his favorite Warped Tour memory? "In 2004, my brother-in-law and I were at the Houston show at the Reliant Arena parking lot. It was probably 101 degrees, and we were checking out the pro skaters on the half-pipe. Afterwards, we were waiting in line to meet the Dropkick Murphys, and we decided then and there to form our own skateboard deck company to make custom decks for bands." Blatant Skateboards has since proudly manufactured decks for the Dropkick Murphys, Big D and the Kids Table, Fear Factory, Kittie, KMFDM, and Rae.

The Band's Experience

What is it like to be in a band on the Vans Warped Tour? In this exclusive interview, Matthew Davies-Kreye, one of the Welsh hard rockers in Funeral for a Friend, talks to the author about the band's first Vans Warped Tour experience, in 2007.

Greg Robison: What was your best experience on the Vans Warped Tour?

Matthew Davies-Kreye, lead singer of Funeral for a Friend, belts it out at a stop on the 2007 Vans Warped Tour. This was the band's first time on the tour.

Matthew Davies-Kreye: Probably playing to a thousand or more kids in Detroit, Michigan. Seeing that many people jumping up and down at the same time to your songs at that time of day (I think it was 12 noon) was breathtaking.

GR: How did the Vans Warped Tour compare to some of your recent European tours?

MDK: It's hard to compare because the Warped Tour is a traveling festival with so many different bands, and Europe doesn't really have any festivals like that . . . Plus, the weather is really different. It's guaranteed to be boiling on Warped Tour, and probably wet and windy at home.

GR: Describe a typical day on tour.

MDK: A typical day usually consists of the tour manager waking you up from your sweet dreams if you happen to have an early set, or just getting up on your own if you are playing later in the day. Then you get cleaned up, have some lunch, and either hang out with some friends or play Xbox 360 on the tour bus. We generally play a twenty-five-minute set, and then do an acoustic set and autograph signings for the kids at one of the vendor booths. After that, it's time to go back on the tour bus, or watch some other bands play before dinner. Then you get some sleep and wake up in another town the next day.

GR: Did you have a favorite city that you played on the tour?

MDK: I really enjoyed playing Denver, Colorado. There was a huge rainstorm that delayed our set for about twenty minutes, and it was an amazing thing to watch. The kids were great—they stuck the weather out and stayed to watch our set.

GR: Do you have any advice for bands that want to play the Vans Warped Tour?

MDK: Be ready to get up at the crack of dawn some days to get your gear ready for your set. Be sure and pack plenty of soap, shampoo, and toilet paper!

The Employee Experience

Working on the Vans Warped Tour is fun, but it's a lot of hard work as well. Sarah Baer of 4Fini, Inc., tells you more about her job in this exclusive interview.

Greg Robison: What is your job title at 4Fini, Inc.?

Sarah Baer: I'm the director of tour marketing and sponsorship. I work with corporate sponsors who want to become involved with the Vans Warped Tour.

GR: What is your favorite part of your job?

SB: I love to people-watch on the Vans Warped Tour, especially the kids watching the bands. It makes all of our hard work worth it when you see everything come together, and all of the kids having such a great time.

GR: What have been some of your favorite bands that you have seen on the Vans Warped Tour?

SB: There are so many, but some of my very favorites have been Joan Jett and the Blackhearts, the Bouncing Souls, Bad Religion, Flogging Molly, Gallows, Paramore, and Gogol Bordello.

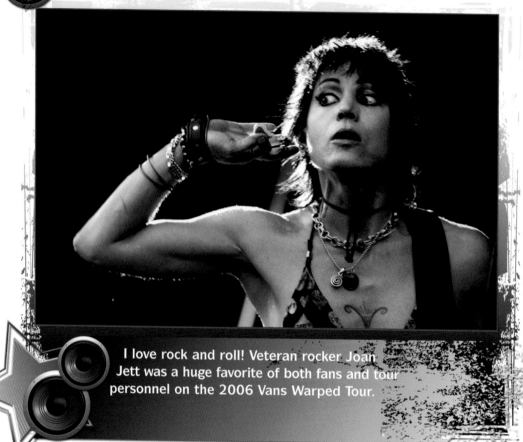

I love rock and roll! Veteran rocker Joan Jett was a huge favorite of both fans and tour personnel on the 2006 Vans Warped Tour.

GR: Do you have any advice for someone who wants to work on the Vans Warped Tour?

SB: You need to be ready to work really hard. There are days on the tour when you will put in sixteen-hour days. It's important to not only love music, but to want to learn the business of music as well.

The Manager Experience

Craig Jennings, cofounder of Raw Power Management, discusses having two of his bands play on the 2007 Warped Tour in this exclusive interview.

Greg Robison: How did you arrange for both Funeral for a Friend and Gallows to appear on the Vans Warped Tour?

Craig Jennings: I know Kevin Lyman [the Vans Warped Tour founder] fairly well. He's a great guy and a big fan of both bands.

GR: Do you feel that the exposure that both bands gained on the tour has been of benefit to them?

CJ: I feel that any band that is fortunate enough to play on the Vans Warped Tour will benefit from the experience and greater exposure—some bands more than others.

GR: What's your overall opinion of the Vans Warped Tour?

CJ: I have had the pleasure of attending the tour several times, and I think it's a fantastic mixture of great bands, both old and new. Additionally, I like the punk rock feel that the Vans Warped Tour has running through it.

CHAPTER 4

HOOK ME UP!

VANS WARPED TOUR TICKETS

You've read about the Vans Warped Tour. You've heard that your favorite band is going to be on the tour. You and your friends have decided, "We're going to the Warped Tour!" That's great and everything—but first, you need to get tickets.

The Vans Warped Tour Web site (www.warpedtour.com) is the best place to begin once you've decided that you want to attend a tour show. Updated all year long, the Web site will keep you aware of who is slated to play on the tour, as well as special tour contests and events. Most important, this is where you can pre-order tickets to the show of your choice, before they even go on sale to the general public. Once the tour routing and lineup is set (generally in late February or early March), this information is posted on the Web site, along with instructions on how to pre-order tickets. Note that if you are planning to pre-order, you will need to pay by credit card. Check back with

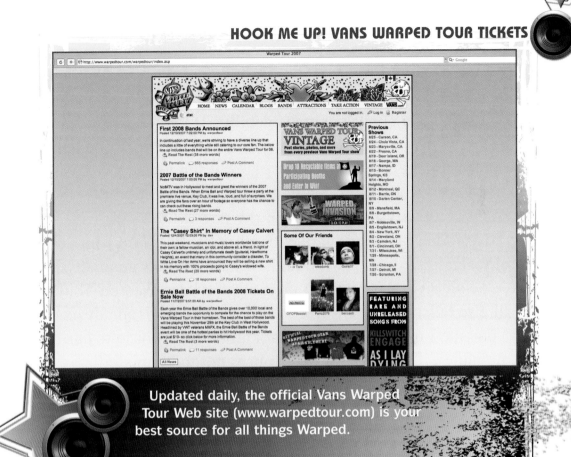

Updated daily, the official Vans Warped Tour Web site (www.warpedtour.com) is your best source for all things Warped.

the Web site often, as there may be contests through which you can win tickets and VIP passes, among other things.

If you are unable to pre-order, you can still get tickets up to the day of the show (provided it doesn't sell out) through Ticketmaster. Check online at www.ticketmaster.com. In addition to the regular price of the ticket, there will be service charges added to all Ticketmaster purchases.

Another ticket source is the box office of the Vans Warped Tour venue. Just give the people at the box office a call, and they can tell you about ticket availability. If you decide at the last minute that you want to go to the show, you might be able to purchase tickets the day of the show at the venue's box office. The Warped Tour generally sells out, but often the venue will release some tickets on the day of the show.

If you don't have the money for a ticket, listen to your local rock/alternative radio stations. These stations generally have ticket giveaways to help promote the Vans Warped Tour. If all else fails, go to your parents and ask them for an advance on your allowance, or do some work around the house to earn extra money. The Vans Warped Tour is not to be missed!

The Future of the Vans Warped Tour

Well over a decade after kicking off the first festival, the Vans Warped Tour is still going strong. One question that its founder Kevin Lyman is asked all the time is how long he thinks the tour will continue. "You know . . . at one point it was never supposed to be ten years," says Lyman. "I never really thought about it when I first started it. Now, I'm like, 'What's wrong with doing this?' As long as the kids keep coming, this is great!" Let's hope that, like Lyman, the Vans Warped Tour keeps going and going.

acoustic Music that is not produced or enhanced electronically.

anticipate To expect or look forward to.

biodiesel Fuel made from vegetable oils or animal fat.

charitable Generous in giving money or helping the needy.

conceive To form a notion or idea of; to imagine.

concession Booth or counter that sells food or beverages at an event.

consultant Person who gives professional or expert advice.

corporation Body of people acting as one for business purposes.

diverse Differing one from another.

emo Type of music influenced by hardcore punk, indie rock, and alternative rock.

genre Type or class.

integral Essential or necessary for completeness.

potential Having possibility, capability, or power.

relevant Having a connection to the matter at hand.

roster Itemized list.

ska Music genre originally from Jamaica.

unflagging Tireless or relentless.

unique Not typical; unusual.

vendor Person or agency that sells.

venture Business undertaking.

venue Scene or locale of any action or event.

FOR MORE INFORMATION

Vans, Inc.
15700 Shoemaker Avenue
Santa Fe Springs, CA 90670
(888) 691-8889
Web site: http://www.vans.com
Vans is the corporate sponsor of the Vans Warped Tour.

Web Sites

Due to the changing nature of Internet links, Rosen Publishing has developed an online list of Web sites related to the subject of this book. This site is updated regularly. Please use this link to access the list:

http://www.rosenlinks.com/mmf/vans

Badillo, Steve, and Doug Werner. *Skateboarding: Book of Tricks.* Chula Vista, CA: Tracks Publishing, 2003.

Browne, David. *Amped: How Big Air, Big Dollars, and a New Generation Took Sports to the Extreme.* New York, NY: Bloomsbury USA, 2005.

Hawk, Tony, and Sean Mortimer. *Hawk: Occupation: Skateboarder.* New York, NY: HarperEntertainment, 2001.

Segovia, Patty, and Rebecca Heller. *Skater Girl: A Girl's Guide to Skateboarding.* Berkeley, CA: Ulysses Press, 2006.

BIBLIOGRAPHY

Alleshouse, Melani. "Warped Mind: An Interview with Warped Tour Founder Kevin Lyman." Utter Trash. Retrieved October 19, 2006 (http://www.uttertrash.net/kevinlyman.htm).

Cuda, Heidi Siegmund, and Chris Gallipoli. *Warped Book: Tales of Freedom and Psychotic Ambition*. South Pasadena, CA: 4 Fini Inc., 2002.

FundingUniverse.com. "Vans, Inc.: Company History." Retrieved November 7, 2007 (http://www.fundinguniverse.com/company-histories/Vans.Inc.-Company-History.html).

Jensen, D. Gabrielle. "Vans Warped Tour: Over a Decade of Music and Extreme Sports and Still Going Strong." Retrieved November 8, 2007 (http://www.associatedcontent.com/article/33339/vans_warped_tour.html).

Live Tour Artists. "Kevin Lyman." Retrieved October 28, 2006 (http://www.livetourartists.com/kevin-lyman).

McDonald, Neil. "Vans Warped Tour, Habitat for Humanity Team Up to Help Hurricane Katrina Victims." 2005. Retrieved November 8, 2007 (http://www.soulshineca/news/newsarticle.php?nid=2609).

TheMusicEdge.com. "Kevin Lyman: Warped Tour Celebrates 10 Successful Years." Retrieved August 19, 2006 (http://www.themusicedge.com/moxie/news/spotartists/kevin-lymanwarped-tour-ce.shtml).

INDEX

About the Author

Greg Robison has been actively involved in the music industry for the past fifteen years. He is the cofounder of an independent record label, has served as a band manager and consultant, and has promoted numerous concerts and special music events. In addition to this title, he is also the author of *Ozzfest*, *Coachella*, and *Christian Rock Festivals*, all published by Rosen Publishing. He and his wife, Kelly, live in Texas.

Photo Credits

Designer: Nelson Sa; Editor: Christopher Roberts
Photo Researcher: Amy Feinberg